WALK WITH WINGS

TENE EDWARDS

The Good Publishing

The Good Quote Publishing

146 Queens Road, Watford, England, WD17 2NX

www.thegood.co

Editor: Carla DuPont Huger and Shayla Raquel

www.shaylaraquel.com

Interior Design: © 2018 Mitch Green

(radpresspublishing@gmail.com)

Book Cover and Illustrations: © 2018 Sarah Faber

(www.sara-faber.com)

ISBN-13: 978-1999588908

Special thanks to Wale Kalejaiye and Meggan Roxanne for taking a chance on me and welcoming me into The Good Quote family.

CONTENTS

I WRITE TO HEAL

Here is the truth about the truth,

it's embarrassing.

We are safe from judgment with the pretense of perfection,

so we lie. Women often carry a weight of

fear, shame, and embarrassment of who we are.

Growing up, I was taught never to air my dirty laundry in

public. However, life has taught me that owning my mistakes

allows me to grab my power back.

And sharing my truth may be the only light others need

to drive them out of their darkness.

To be free and to free others, I write my truth.

Welcome to my truth.

1.
MONSOON LOVE

LOVESTRUCK

I had my guard up,

but your kiss to my soul brought that barrier down.

And, when I fell asleep smiling that night

for the first time in a long time...

I knew that had to mean something.

YOUR VOICE

It's late and I'm tired,

but still I wait on your call.

Your voice is the medication

for the frustration with the distance.

Your voice is my brightest sunshine

through the winter nights.

Your voice is the only melody

that can rock me to sleep.

MISSING YOU

Another night,

another ache for you.

As I lay on my bed,

I scroll through my phone,

get lost in watching you.

And wonder if you watch me, too.

SYNCHRONIZATION

Isn't it strange that two people could be awake at 3.00 a.m. thinking about each other, but have no idea?

THE FALL

She fell in love with a bad boy
because he brought out the wild in her
and it felt like freedom.

ATTACHMENT

I inhaled your scent and got high as fuck.

FOREVER

I was never strong enough to leave.

Not even an earthquake could have kept me away.

I would have chanced the jump for you.

I was willing to hold on

for as long as you wanted me to stay,

because I said forever,

and I meant it.

LOVE CAREFULLY

You cannot help whom you fall for,

but be careful who you choose to love.

WINTER SORROW

BAD BOYS

She only warns you away from bad boys

because she has danced with one herself.

She knows how addictive they are,

and how difficult withdrawal symptoms get.

BLINDED BY LOVE

Your touch struck me like lightning;

it set my heart on fire, but paralyzed my brain.

LOVE BLIND

They say, "follow your heart,"

but sometimes the heart can be unreliable

when it tangles in the blindness of love.

CAN'T LET GO

How many stabs is it going to take

for me to realize my worth?

Every chance I give, you wreck.

Every promise you make, you break.

You always leave, and I burst into tears.

If anyone knew the things you put me through,

they'd probably say that I was insane

for staying with the person

who owns the knife to my wounds.

Love is not an excuse, but love is the only reason.

TRUE COLORS

The promises were sweet,

but your actions grew sour.

CONSEQUENCES

Just because he craves you

does not mean he wants to pursue you.

Think about your value before you pay the price.

INTUITION

I don't like to gamble,

but if there is one thing I am willing to bet on,

it's my intuition.

Because how can I distrust my gut

when it has never failed me?

REVEALING SIGNS

Don't be fooled by someone's promises

when their actions often contradict their words.

Playing blind to the truth is self-abuse.

You know your worth - I know you do.

So trust the signs - they speak the truth.

FRUSTRATION

Nothing is more painful

than having to watch something that kills you

with no authority to say anything,

because of the position you have chosen to settle in.

ABOLISHED

Your T-shirt was my favourite pajama,

and I protected your gift like treasure;

but when you broke me, I broke it

and disposed of everything that reminded me of you.

DYING LOVE

I stopped trying to figure out what went wrong

when I realized that it was always wrong

and could never get right.

For what was the worth in fighting

to keep alive a love

that died a long time ago?

ALMOST RIGHT

You were almost right.

You had most of the qualities

I had been looking for.

You showed me things I had never seen before.

I saw the potential in you,

I saw the potential in us,

I overcame the dirt you branded as mistakes,

and although it was difficult, I thought it would be worth it.

But you just kept repeating them, time and time again.

You clearly could not help yourself.

It almost could have worked, but that bad quality

outweighed all the good.

Almost was never enough.

CAGED

Sometimes the memories come back to haunt me,

and I drive myself crazy.

Questioning the things you said,

questioning where we went wrong,

questioning what that moment meant to you.

I understand why caged animals often fight to escape.

REMINISCING

I miss the way you loved me,

but I don't want you back,

because the way you crushed me,

I will never forget.

FUCKBOYS

Being a good woman in a world full of fuckboys
is the realest struggle I have ever known.

FATHERS

Fathers should endeavor to prove

that good men still exist

by teaching their daughters

how a woman should be treated

through leading by example.

HEARTBREAK

It takes strength to forgive without closure.

Only when you left me broken, I found self-love.

Heartbreak is a brutal teacher.

BROKEN ANGEL

She's just a strong woman with a weak heart.

Sweet, though broken.

She's an angel in a black dress.

TRUST ISSUES

Her father was her last hope

for proving good men still exist.

It was only when he let her down

that she became skeptical of love.

STILL I DREAM

I have risked my pride,

risked my heart,

risked abandoning my own needs,

for a shot at the fairytale dream,

and lost.

Opening to love has always been a gamble,

and although I have lost at every shot,

still I dream.

YOU ARE ENOUGH

You are enough,

you always have been.

Just not for him, but for the man meant for you.

DIFFERENT

My mother knew I was gonna be different
the day she named me.

HAPPINESS

Happiness seemed unreachable.

The lows became a weight too heavy to carry,

and your impatience took a toll on you.

You were tired of waiting for the next high,

so you intoxicated yourself to achieve this.

The satisfying release became an addiction,

but the numbness was only temporary.

We spend so much time chasing happiness

that we fail to appreciate what we already have now.

Take a look around you.

You can breathe, can't you?

You are still loved, aren't you?

You are bound to find something valuable

hiding in a skip of junk.

DISCIPLINE

Practice the discipline of gratitude
in both the good times and the bad.

PRACTICE GRATITUDE

Some days I feel like crying,

some days I feel lonely and lost.

Some days I feel ugly,

and some days I feel everything at once.

But the practice of gratitude

has taught me how to glow through the dark.

BLESSINGS

Be grateful for the things you are able to do,

and for the loved ones you are able to see.

MEMORY TRIGGERS

Some past mistakes live on your skin
as beautiful memory triggers for the moans
you should have absorbed, but ignored.
Like the sound of your mother's voice
every time you look at that permanent scar
you could have avoided, if only you had listened.

OWN WHO YOU ARE

Never allow anyone to determine

how much of a beautiful woman you are

by the features on your face,

the shade of your skin,

or the size of your body.

You don't need anyone's approval

to feel good about the way you look.

You determine how much

of a beautiful woman you are.

Make your heart the most beautiful feature you carry,

because outer beauty is only skin deep.

BODY CONFIDENCE

I began to value my body more
when I stopped focusing on the flaws,
and started to appreciate everything
that it allows me to do.

A LETTER TO MY NATURAL HAIR

I am sorry I neglected you, abused and abandoned you.
Permed from an age so young, I can't even remember
the first time that stick full of toxins touched and ruined
you. I was taught straight, soft hair was the only style of
beauty, so with my relaxer and straighteners, I continued
to destroy you. For all these years, I believed long, thick
hair could only be hereditary. I wear extensions, weaves
and wigs to hide the real you. I am embarrassed of you. I
am sorry I took no care of you. I knew no better, but I now
know better; for I am learning to accept you, care for and
nourish you. I know I still do not show you; I am working
on my love for you... preparing for the day that I will flaunt
and cherish you.

BODY POSITIVE

To all the women struggling to love their looks,

let me ask you something:

who are you comparing yourselves to?

Why is it that

we spend more time admiring the beauty in others,

and not cherishing the beauty within ourselves?

Let's stop searching

for our beauty in the compliments of others,

and practice appreciating the magic living within us.

NATURE

As my relationship with God strengthens,
my appreciation for His art increases.

BREAST CANCER : SCARRED SURVIVOR

My breasts are not the same,
said my mother
as she looked down at them and frowned.

How terrifying it must have been
to hear that such a deadly disease
had invited itself in,
trespassed on your breast
and vandalized it before it left.

Find the beauty in imperfection,
I answered.

This scar is not a punishment,
but an award for your strength and bravery.

Don't you dare allow it to torture you.
I don't want you to let it haunt you.
Cherish the way it sits on your skin
as a warrior mark, signifying survivor.

Let this scar be a reminder of your victory.

WALK WITH GRACE

If you are unable to find the blessings

on the step that you are currently stuck on,

be prepared to live a life of misery.

Only when you walk with grace

will you taste the sweetness of happiness.

PEACE

Hate cannot access my heart,

for it is securely protected with peace.

CELEBRATE YOURSELF

Stop criticizing yourself over the things you haven't done,
and start celebrating the things that you have achieved.

GRACE

The journey of life

meets sadness, as well as happiness;

greet both seasons with grace.

TEACH OTHERS

Learn how to love yourself,

then teach others how it's done.

We rise not only by lifting others, but

by speaking our truth.

REJECTION

Tired of rejection?

So am I.

Maybe one day our time will come.

But as for now,

we must keep giving the best we can.

We must stay loyal to the faith in ourselves.

Rejection will not discourage us,

because the hunger to achieve

outcraves the fear of failure.

TAKE NOTE

When you're feeling like a failure,

remember the grenades you have crushed,

the setbacks you have overcome,

and the battles you have won.

This journey through life is rough, I know,

but still with courage, you climb.

This strength you have built will take you places.

Be proud of the warrior you have become.

UNDEFEATABLE

There will be those who will try to drag you down
because of their own insecurities that they let consume them.
No matter what, stay crafting.

TRUST IN GOD

I know times may be hard for you right now,

but feed your mind some affirmations

and let God deal with it.

INDESTRUCTIBLE

It took blood, sweat, and tears to bring me

this far up the mountain of self-love.

Not a single soul is ever again able to defeat me;

this back I have built is indestructible.

GIRL POWER

She's watching you thinking you're doing better.

You're watching her thinking she's doing better.

Instead of supporting each other,

we're wrestling each other.

Women need to start empowering each other.

We grow stronger when we stand together.

HOLD THE VISION

Life as a creative is a mountain trek.

It takes determination and willpower,

courage and discipline.

You must hold the vision tightly

and trust the process fiercely;

despite the emails full of junk,

or pockets full of dust.

It is your responsibility to persist through the fog.

MIND GAMES

If you approach the mountain in fear,

it will look bigger than it actually is.

BE BRAVE

You can train as hard as you like,
but you will never know your strengths
until you face the ring.

S E L F - D O U B T

Today, I am losing hope,
my inner critic is chanting at me.

"You are not good enough."
"Everyone is laughing at you."
"Remember the insults."

Today, the disturbing condition
of chronic self-doubt
may be at an all-time high,
but I ought to remember
that even the greatest leaders
stumble upon it.

I must not allow it to beat me,
since it is only just part of the process.

VOW FOR SUCCESS

She's a lady on a mission,

married to the grind.

For better,

for worse,

for richer,

for poorer,

in sickness and in health,

until death do her part.

KEEP ROLLING

There are only so many times you can roll a dice,
before it lands on a six.

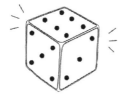

SELF-CONFIDENCE

She is going to win,

even if they don't want her to.

She may run into a setback,

but will break through with a comeback,

because hustlers never give up;

they keep going.

STAY

I may not be perfect, but at least I give my best.

I ask but one thing of you, and only one

"Don't give up on me, no matter what."

Just be down forever.

SELF-BELIEF

The grind is tough,

but worth every sweat.

I believe in the woman I am striving to become.

GRIND

There are only so many times you can flip a coin

before it lands on the other side.

GIRL BOSS

Just an independent woman,

building my empire from the ground up.

HUSTLE OVER LUCK

"You're so lucky; you always get what you want." Am I? I don't always get what I want. Just because I walk with a smile, you assume my life is always sparkly bright. As if I have never soaked in rain and stumbled over hurdles, time and time again. As if I have never crumbled in pain, and strained myself out the drain. As if I don't have problems of my own; I do. My attitude is just different. I carry grace with me wherever I tread, wherever I hang and wherever I land. I have hustled for everything I have right now; luck is not something I believe in.

SELF-BRANDING

Your mind is your lead,

inject it with positivity.

Your feet are your foundation,

walk with purpose.

And your heart is your stamp,

make it beautiful.

V.

SUMMER FREEDOM

BROKEN BUT CHOSEN

I craved your love and sacrificed myself.

You craved my body and dumped me when you were fed.

You played me, but I found my worth.

You chose her, but the universe chose me;

to transmute my pain into art.

You flaunt her while I flaunt my success.

You gave up on me, but I leveled up on you.

So, thank you for stabbing my heart,

I needed the pain to birth my art.

FOREVER QUEEN

I don't care about who you've been with,

desired to be with,

or left me to get with,

because no other woman can intimidate me.

SURVIVOR

My tears built the ocean that you brutally threw me in.

When you left me to drown,

I grew the strength to float.

Bravely learned how to swim,

and saved myself at the shore.

WOMAN OF STRENGTH

I have never met a strong woman

who has never been broken.

She had to learn

how to pick herself up and carry on.

She had to learn

how to depend on herself for happiness.

UNFORGETTABLE

Miss me? Of course you do.

Did you honestly think I'd be easy to forget?

You imprisoned yourself, but set me free.

I gave you the best of me,

yet you dragged out the worst in me.

You should have known better.

And maybe I should have known better, too.

IRREPLACEABLE

Nobody

has the same heartprint as you.

LOVE HURTS

I know what it's like to be sold a dream of a forever ring
and a couple of kids that you have already
discussed the names of. How someone can be warm
today, yet cold tomorrow. When deep talk turns into
small talk and love bites fade into bitter lies. I know what
it's like to lose yourself to the drug of love. I know how
it feels to be confused about love, to be confused about
your feelings, to be confused about life. I know how it
feels to be taken for granted, to be taken for a fool, to be
taken advantage of. Nobody is exempt from heartbreak.
You may have been the best thing that happened to
them, but they were not the best thing that happened to
you. You may have lost the man you loved, but now you
are free to receive the man you deserve.

SHIT HAPPENS

Every now and then, life will throw obstacles at you.

Duck or dive if you want to,

but you won't be able to dodge them all the time.

You will get hit,

you will stumble,

you will fall,

and there is nothing you can do about it.

You cannot control what life hits you with,

but you can control how you deal with it.

Self-pity will leave you stranded.

Misery will leave you grounded.

Sometimes you have to cut your losses,

and keep moving on.

FAITH

I have never doubted God's plan,

I wholeheartedly trust in His timing.

INNER BATTLES

If you're fighting against yourself because of a mistake

that goes against your morals,

let me tell you something...

We have all done something we never thought we'd do.

A slip-up doesn't make you any less of a good woman.

FREE YOURSELF

Don't allow your mistakes to leave you tied up.

Untangle the knot and set yourself free from the past.

SURVIVAL

You've traveled through so much pain,

you can't help but see

the clouds before the storm,

the rain before it pours,

the dark before dawn.

Assuming the worst will be the death of you.

Hope it 'til you hear it.

Force it 'til you feel it.

Crave it 'til you taste it.

And dream it 'til you own it.

That is how I survived.

Awaken your soul.

SITUATIONSHIP

Back at it again with the guy you're supposed to be over.

You know he's no good,

but still you feed him attention.

You sacrifice your needs to satisfy his.

Sometimes you want to call him,

but you're scared he won't be there,

because majority of the time he is busy and absent.

Now you question yourself:

to swim with the shark or away from the risk?

If you find yourself trapped in a situationship,

stop giving too much of yourself away.

Let him prove to you he's worth the risk.

TREAT ME RIGHT

Look at you!

Strutting around in your fancy gear, hunting validation.

Am I supposed to be flattered?

Am I supposed to be impressed?

Well, I couldn't care less about your diamond watch;

material things will never excite me.

I applaud the richness of loyalty and respect.

For nothing is more attractive

than a man with self-control and discipline.

INNER BEAUTY

I just hope your heart shines as bright
as the materialistic things you flaunt.

RE-EVALUATION

If you are more in love with the man he used to be,

than the man he has now unmasked to be,

maybe it's time to face the truth.

I understand that you stay for all the things

he has done right,

but sometimes the wrongs outweigh the rights.

DIGNITY

Be brave enough to walk away
and wait for someone to treat you right,
before you end up giving your whole self
to a heartless stranger.

ACCOMPANY YOURSELF

Sometimes you have to crawl through a little loneliness

in order to bump into someone who will accompany you

toward finding your feet to dance again.

And don't be surprised if that somebody is you.

Because being alone will never

outburn the loneliness grieved in the wrong relationship.

KNOW YOUR WORTH

You might miss out on a chance at love
by being in your feelings for the wrong one.

N O W   O R   N E V E R

I will only reveal my feelings once - take it or leave it.

I've wasted too much time waiting around;

it's either now or never.

If you don't want to aid my heart, don't abuse my feelings.

If you don't want to love me, don't expect me to stay.

Your stab may wound my heart, but it cannot kill my power to

love. I don't need you to appreciate me;

I'll find someone who will.

Now don't you dare pity me;

I can handle the truth.

You can't hurt my self-esteem,

my self-love is firm.

SELF-LOVE

I don't need you to love me,

I love me.

LOVE EXISTS

There will come a time
when you will love someone,
who won't love you back.
There will also come a time
when someone will love you,
who you won't love back.
But there will come a time
when you will love someone,
who will love you back.

SOMEONE'S FAVORITE

One day you will be someone's favorite shell.

Your face will be their favourite sight.

And they will fall in love with the way you're designed.

GOODBYE

You walked away, now you're walking back.

Why is that?

If you are going to go, stay gone.

I am fed up with your hot-and-cold attitude,

and I am done with biting my tongue.

I am not going to be that girl anymore,

who remains quiet for peace.

I will speak my mind because I value myself,

and I am done with you taking advantage of me.

Your fabricated stories, I no longer have time for.

I've got more important things to do.

I have goals to achieve and places to be.

If you cannot respect me, expect me to leave.

SELF-AFFIRMATION

I will never settle for less than I deserve;

I know my worth.

LOVE YOURSELF

The plan to ignore you back has failed once again. I scorn
broken promises, yet struggle to fulfill some I make to myself.
Why can't I be strong enough to do you how you do me? I
spoke to myself and I told myself that I was done with you. I
rehearsed my lines, was ready to perform, yet the moment
you called, I caught stage fright. By no surprise, I forgot my
lines, and of course threw myself back into the spinning
wheel again. I devalued my worth, which tortured my soul,
but I only have myself to blame. Now I don't know how,
but I know somehow I am finding the strength to move on.
Because I am a queen, I am loved by me, and I refuse to let a
man make a toy out of me.

FIGHTING TEMPTATION

Tired of him running back and forth,

you no longer want to be an option.

If you are fighting the temptation to return,

here is what you can do:

I. Write down a list of all the reasons this person is not for you.

2. Write down a list next to it of all the qualities you want in a

partner that this person lacked.

3. When temptation knocks, read it over. Again and again. Let it

sink deep down into your mind.

LAPSE OF TIME

As new chapters are born, old chapters die.

Everything ceases at some point.

I know it's sad, but life goes on.

- nothing, nothing is forever

NO DIFFERENT

Just as I started feeling you, here we go again...

the lies, empty promises, games, and similar ways;

I just can't seem to find my way out this gloomy maze.

I'm stringing onto hope, but frozen at a dead end.

I thought you were different, but you spun around the same.

I thought you'd be the one, but my prediction was wrong.

I thought I gave up on love, but you came along.

You proved how much I crave it,

but I'm not willing to settle.

I never loved you, but I wanted to.

I never admitted my feelings, but I wanted to.

I wanted to, but I never.

I was waiting for you, but you never.

Now I'll never know how you felt about me,

but that no longer matters.

You showed me all I needed to know,

and that is why we shattered.

INTROVERT

Her persona may be quiet,
but her observation loud.

I DESERVE

I deserve to be loved.

I deserve to be happy.

I deserve to be appreciated and treated with respect.

I am tired of fighting my depression over you.

I am tired of settling for what I don't deserve.

I am done with treading on broken glass.

I give up on tolerating less than my worth.

Now I'm dropping anyone who disturbs my peace.

And I'm blocking anyone who makes me feel unwanted.

I'm slashing my way out of toxic relationships,

and asserting my dignity and pride.

For I am saving all my love for someone who proves

that they're loyal and down to ride.

GOD'S PLAN

God would never take what is meant for you,
away from you.

GOOD RIDDANCE

I knew I had to leave.

I was tired of feeling empty and forcing sleep

to escape the pain of feeling unloved and unworthy.

I was giving too much of myself,

and not receiving enough.

I was depriving myself of happiness,

and not smiling enough.

I was floating along with feelings,

but had to jump off with pride.

Moving on for the better, ready for something better.

KEEP IT MOVING

Do not allow his misbehavior to dominate your mind.

Keep it moving, baby girl.

SELF-HEALING

You will keep forgiving the one you love

until the day you wake up and hate them.

But in order to heal, you must learn how to forgive again.

Not for them, but for yourself.

Do it for yourself.

LETTING GO

Blocked,

unblocked,

deleted,

then installed,

but at the moment, blocked.

I had to cut off all contact

to get my mind right.

I had to check myself

before I lost myself.

I distanced myself to seek myself.

And when I found myself,

I lost my appetite for you.

- taste buds change

SELF-CARE

As of lately,

I've been busy just taking care of me.

DEAR SELF

I apologize for torturing you with the negative self-talk I exposed you to. I apologize for being ashamed of you for the mistakes you have made... you're only human too. Still learning and growing. Breathing and changing. Falling and climbing. I forgive you for the lies you have told, in the darkness of mourning when you were afraid of your truth. I forgive you for the bitter thoughts you carried before you found healing for your bruise. You are a beautiful woman, a respectful, powerful, and fearless woman. I am proud of you for the hurdles you have jumped to secure the blessings you have today, and I am proud of you for staying strong through your growth from a girl to a lady. Today these words may not sink in, but one day they will if you repeat them daily.

WALK WITH KINDNESS

Be mindful of your reactions to the people

who have wronged you.

You cannot discharge bad energy

and expect good in return.

Anger is never an excuse to be bitter.

There is never an excuse for sin.

I challenge you not to grant anyone the power

to destroy the beauty of your pure heart.

I dare you not to wrong others,

for the way they have wronged you.

You are better than that.

You are kinder than that.

What good will two wrongs make?

R A D I A N T

Throw stones if you wish,

but no amount of cruelty

can destroy the kindness in me

for I am a candlelight

incapable of blowing out.

EVALUATION

Torn between giving it another shot or letting go?

Skeptical about whether you are making the right decision,

or the wrong decision?

Wondering if you should jump or remain put?

Unsure as to whether you want to seize the opportunity,

or leave the opportunity to slip away?

You will find your answer after you have weighed up

the pros and the cons.

LIFE IS SHORT

If you feel like you've had enough,

why don't you set yourself free?

Travel the world.

Face your fears.

Practice forgiveness.

Make yourself happy.

You never know when your time is up.

Now is the time to live.

CONTROL

It is not because of your surroundings that you are trapped.

It is not because of a mistake that you are stranded.

It is not because of others that you are immobile.

It is simply because of you.

You can waste time blaming others for your distress,

or you can accept responsibility for your actions.

You can place the remote to your happiness

in someone else's hand,

or you can take control and change the channel.

STAY KIND

It takes strength to preserve a good soul

in a world full of evil,

but that competence will reward you in due time.

Stay kind.

UNAPOLOGETIC

You think you know me, but you don't. How do you supposedly know me when I don't even fully know myself? I know my capabilities and I know my worth, but sometimes I surprise myself. I have done things that I am not proud of. And although I cannot right my wrongs, I can improve my future. I have achieved many things I never thought were possible. I am still learning to love myself. I am still learning new things about myself. And for as long as I have breath, my story remains under construction. I am a good woman, not an angel... of course, I sin too. But yet, still, with all of the setbacks, the comebacks, the rejections, and the achievements, I am proud of the woman I am becoming.

TRIAL AND ERROR

You strengthen your confidence

through trial and error.

Your mistakes will shape you

into a stronger version of yourself.

I AM WHO I AM

Judge me if you want to,

but I am who I am

and your approval is worthless.

NOBODY'S BUSINESS

You have no authority to judge someone

who sins differently than you.

How others choose to live their life is nobody's business.

CHANGES

There will come a time in your life

when you will take the wrong turn,

miss your stop,

or be forced to take another route.

You will have no idea where this new path may lead to.

And that is the beauty of life.

The aftermath of an error is unpredictable,

your future life is undeterminable,

you cannot prepare for the unforeseeable,

but trusting the universe is feasible.

Your comfort zone will only obstruct you;

brave the challenge of change.

SELF-DEVELOPMENT

Don't be afraid
to rebrand yourself.

UNDEFEATABLE

I was trapped in a cage,

lost in the dark - praying for a way out.

Hope was all I had and I gripped onto it,

like a Pit bull with a lockjaw.

My soul was tired and my strength had weakened. Rather

than sitting down lost in hope,

I knew I had to do something.

So I gave that punch bag the hardest hit I could possibly give,

and on came my breakthrough.

The leash had snapped and I was ready to hunt

for everything I deserve.

Refusing to settle for less,

nothing or nobody could tame me.

WILD AT HEART

Brave girl, you were made for the wild...
don't allow society to tame you on its leash.

MOVING FORWARD

I will not allow you

to guilt-trip me into believing that

forgiveness requires offering you another chance.

I have accepted the fact that

mistakes are entwined in the cycle of life.

And I have cleansed my heart

from all anger, bitterness, and hatred.

I am forgiving you for my own peace of mind,

and if that requires evicting you from my space,

then so be it.

It is not about you anymore.

I am doing this for myself.

COMMITMENT

If you want me around,

but I'm not good enough for your commitment,

stay lonely on your own,

for you are not worthy of my love.

FORGIVENESS

Maturity has taught me to accept that everyone makes

mistakes, including myself. I, therefore, forgive anyone who has

wronged me, even those who have never delivered an apology. I

find it difficult to express myself and maybe

you had no idea how much your actions were hurting me.

I know that I am difficult to understand...most introverts are.

Sometimes I want to be alone, sit in sadness, and cry on my

own. And when I do, I wipe my tears before anyone sees me. For

I have mastered the skill of forcing a smile when others come

around in moments of unhappiness. I always choose to mask

the pain rather than to risk the burden being passed on-to

somebody else. I do not want anybody to feel guilty

for hurting me, and I do not want anybody to feel guilty

for not being there to comfort me. Because sadness lasts

only a moment, and all moments pass. I am learning to open

up more, for I have grown to understand that I cannot expect

people to treat me the way I desire, if I do not teach them how

to by communicating my feelings. I am understanding that not

everybody will treat me the way I want to be treated, or love

me the way I need. But I have learned how to value my worth,

and will continue to value my worth, regardless.

VOWS TO SELF

But when the war was over,
I came back to my senses and
made a vow to myself:
"I'm gonna love me better."

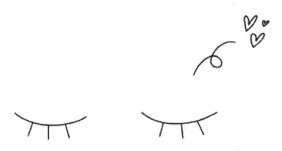

I AM ALL I NEED

I don't need you to believe in me,

I believe in me.

I don't need you to value me,

I value me.

I would never beg you for attention,

I can feed that shit to myself.

I never needed you,

I wanted you.

I can satisfy my own needs.

LOVE AGAIN

Don't tell me you give up on love
when Cupid is plotting to strike you,
and don't tell me your heart is cold
when you warm the hearts of others.

PARTNERSHIP

I crave a love that adds value to my life.

I don't want a relationship,

I want a partnership.

Someone to aid me up the mountain of life

and guide me through the valleys of adversity.

Someone who is able to breathe in sync

and dance by my side through thick and thin.

I want that grind-together type of love,

with a best friend I can build an empire beside.

GOD CAME THROUGH

I thank God for removing the toxic people
from my life,
in the times when I could not find the strength
to remove them myself.

MY SAFE PLACE

As of lately,

it's just been me and God.

He knows all my secrets

and all my hopes and dreams.

He is who I turn to

when I am feeling lonely,

when I am afraid,

and when I lose myself.

So the next time you wonder

why I share so little,

I want you to understand that God is my safe place.

WISDOM

"Uncle, what do you find so savory about oyster
and mussel?"

"I don't eat them for their taste,
I eat them for their value,"

I applied this wisdom to my daily actions,
and it improved my life for the better.

I AM

Today, I affirm that I am worthy of inner peace.

I did not come this far only to settle for mediocrity.

No longer will I entertain toxic things.

Today, I affirm that I am strong and powerful.

I accept my imperfections

and I do not need anyone to validate me.

Today, I affirm that I will pick up my broken pieces

and transform them into wings, because after everything

I have been through, I deserve to be happy.

And so, from this day forward, I will walk with wings.

Instagram, Twitter, Facebook, Tumblr

@teneedwards

Printed in Poland
by Amazon Fulfillment
Poland Sp. z o.o., Wrocław